THE
Fantastic
CUTAWAY BOOK OF
FLIGHT

JON RICHARDS *AND* ALEX PANG

COPPER BEECH BOOKS

BROOKFIELD, CONNECTICUT

Created by David West
and Alex Pang for
Aladdin Books Ltd
28 Percy Street
London W1P 0LD

First published in
the United States in 1998 by
Copper Beech Books,
an imprint of
The Millbrook Press
2 Old New Milford Road
Brookfield, Connecticut
06804

Printed in Belgium

Editor
Simon Beecroft
Consultant
Colin Uttley
Design
David West
Children's Book Design
Designer
Robert Perry
Picture research
Brooks Krikler Research
Illustrators
Alex Pang
and Ross Watton

Library of Congress
Cataloging-in-Publication Data
Richards, Jon, 1970-
The fantastic cutaway book of
flight / by Jon Richards; illustrated
by Alex Pang and Ross Watton.
p. cm.
Includes index.
Summary: Cross-section
illustrations reveal the complex
technology of 747s, helicopters,
supersonic jets, and other
vehicles of flight.
ISBN 0-7613-0719-2 (lib. bdg.)
ISBN 0-7613-0726-5 (pb)
1. Aeronautics—Juvenile literature.
2. Airplanes—Juvenile literature.
[1. Airplanes. 2. Aeronautics.]
I. Pang, Alex, ill. II. Watton,
Ross, ill. III. Title.
TL547.R46 1998   97-43127
629.13—dc21   CIP AC
5 4 3 2 1

CONTENTS

INTRODUCTION

For centuries, people have yearned to soar through the air. However, true powered flight has only become a reality in the last hundred years. In the short time since then we have built a dazzling array of flying machines that perform a huge number of roles. They can be hot-air balloons that are flown for fun, huge passenger jets that carry people around the world, helicopters that hover over our cities, or sleek fighter planes that are used in the more serious business of war.

Throughout their development, aircraft have always used the most advanced technology. Whether this is the lightest engines fitted to the first powered planes or the highly advanced design of today's "invisible" Stealth Bomber, aircraft have been involved in pushing back the boundaries of development. This means that today we can board a huge jet plane that will take us to the other side of the world in a matter of hours.

THE DAWN OF FLIGHT

DA VINCI'S ORNITHOPTER

For centuries, some of the world's greatest inventors have tried to design aircraft.
During the early 1500s, the Italian artist Leonardo da Vinci made drawings of human-powered flying machines called ornithopters (above). However, all these machines would have been too heavy to fly. By the late 1800s, the German inventor Otto Lilienthal built several gliders (right) that proved controllable flight was possible. Eventually, the critical moment came in the early 1900s with the development of a light engine that could power planes into the air.

LILIENTHAL'S GLIDER

DU TEMPLE'S STEAM PLANE

French inventor Felix du Temple designed many planes during the last half of the 19th century. This aircraft (below), built in 1857, was powered by a steam engine and had many advanced features, including retractable landing gear. It was too heavy to get off the ground. However, in 1874, du Temple achieved success when another of his steam-powered planes made a short, powered, flying hop.

DU TEMPLE'S STEAM PLANE

THE PHILLIPS I

The bizarre-looking Phillips I (right), designed by the English inventor Horatio Phillips, had 21 narrow wings joined together to form a "lifting frame" – although it looked more like a venetian blind! This aircraft was built in 1904. Phillips later modified it and then claimed to have made a powered flight of 500 ft (150 m) – although this was never proved.

THE PHILLIPS I

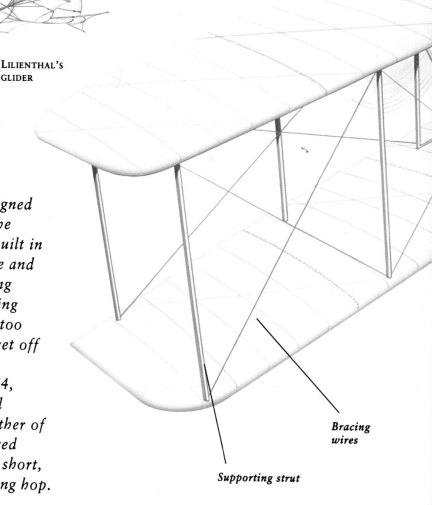

Propeller

Bracing wires

Supporting strut

LOUIS BLÉRIOT

On July 25, 1909, the French aviator Louis Blériot (below) took off from the north coast of France to become the first person to fly a plane across the English Channel. He was flying in response to a competition set up by the English newspaper the Daily Mail. His plane, the Blériot XI (right), was a monoplane and it made the 24-mile (38-km) journey in under 40 minutes.

BLÉRIOT XI

LOUIS BLÉRIOT

Engine

Pilot

THE WRIGHT BROTHERS

The distinction of flying the first powered, controllable plane went to two bicycle manufacturers from the United States, Wilbur and Orville Wright. On December 17, 1903, at Kitty Hawk, North Carolina, Orville Wright made the first flight, which lasted only 12 seconds! The plane, the Wright Flyer I (left), had the pilot balanced on the lower wing between two propellers. Sadly, the Flyer I was damaged on the final landing that day and was then wrecked when a gust of wind flipped it over.

WRIGHT FLYER I

SIKORSKY LE GRAND

One of the great figures in aviation history was the Ukranian-born Igor Sikorsky. In 1913, he built the enormous "Le Grand" (right). It was the world's first passenger plane and the largest aircraft of its day. Passengers traveled in luxury with armchairs, a sofa, and a bathroom. Sikorsky later emigrated to the United States where he turned his attention to helicopters (see page 20).

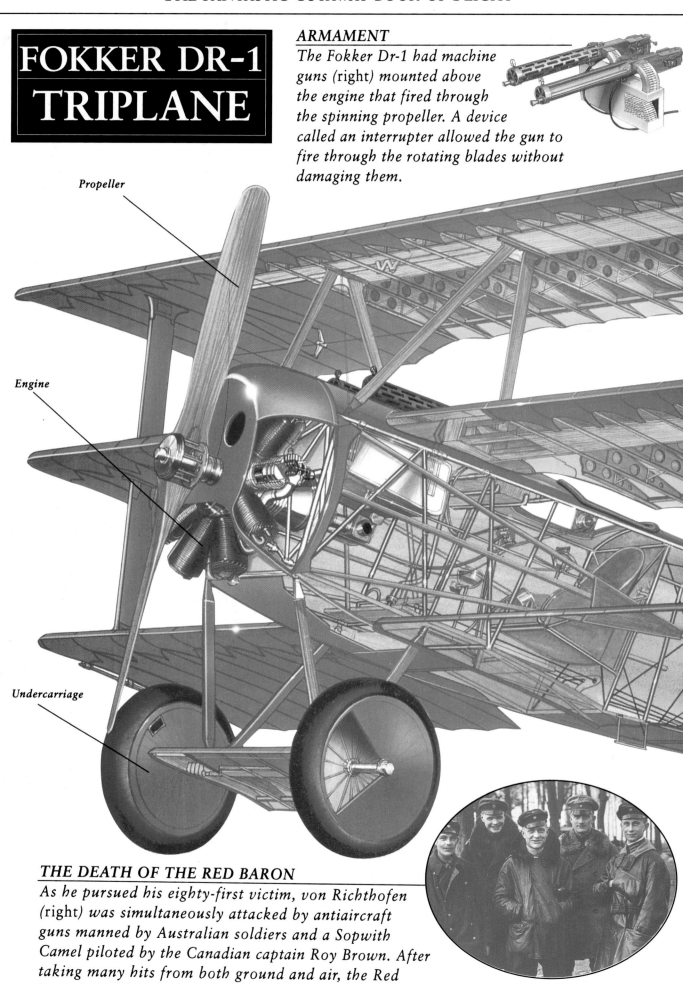

FOKKER DR-1 TRIPLANE

ARMAMENT

The Fokker Dr-1 had machine guns (right) mounted above the engine that fired through the spinning propeller. A device called an interrupter allowed the gun to fire through the rotating blades without damaging them.

Propeller

Engine

Undercarriage

THE DEATH OF THE RED BARON

As he pursued his eighty-first victim, von Richthofen (right) was simultaneously attacked by antiaircraft guns manned by Australian soldiers and a Sopwith Camel piloted by the Canadian captain Roy Brown. After taking many hits from both ground and air, the Red Baron's Fokker Dr-1 plunged to the ground and crashed.

THE RED BARON (CENTER)

ENGINE POWER

The Fokker Dr-1 was powered by an Oberursel rotary engine. This engine could propel the Fokker Dr-1 to a speed of 115 mph (185 km/h).

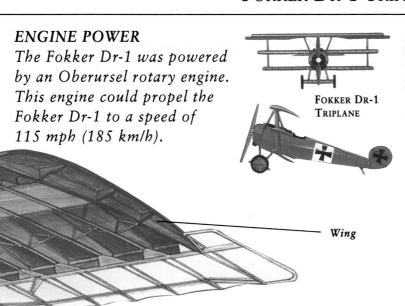

FOKKER DR-1 TRIPLANE

Wing

WORLD WAR I was the first conflict to see aircraft fighting each other in the skies. At first, pilots flew clumsy machines, but by the end of the war aircraft companies were producing fast and agile planes, such as the Fokker Dr-1 triplane. This was flown by one of the greatest pilots of the war, the German Baron Manfred von Richthofen. Before he was killed in April 1918, he had shot down 80 aircraft. Richthofen was nicknamed the Red Baron after the color of his planes. His squadron, Jagdstafel II, also flew brightly colored aircraft and were known by Allied pilots as the "Flying Circus."

THREE WINGS

The short wings of the Fokker Dr-1 made the plane very maneuverable. To compensate for the shortness of its wings the aircraft needed three of them to give it enough lift to fly. Another World War I aircraft that had three wings was the British Sopwith Triplane.

Tail skid

SOPWITH CAMEL

The war's finest fighter was the Sopwith Camel (right). Its speed and maneuverability made it a supreme fighter and, with 2,790 victories, it shot down more planes than any other aircraft during the war. It was named after the hump above the engines that housed the guns.

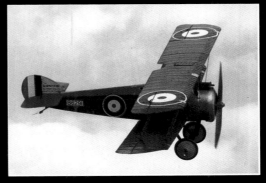

SOPWITH CAMEL

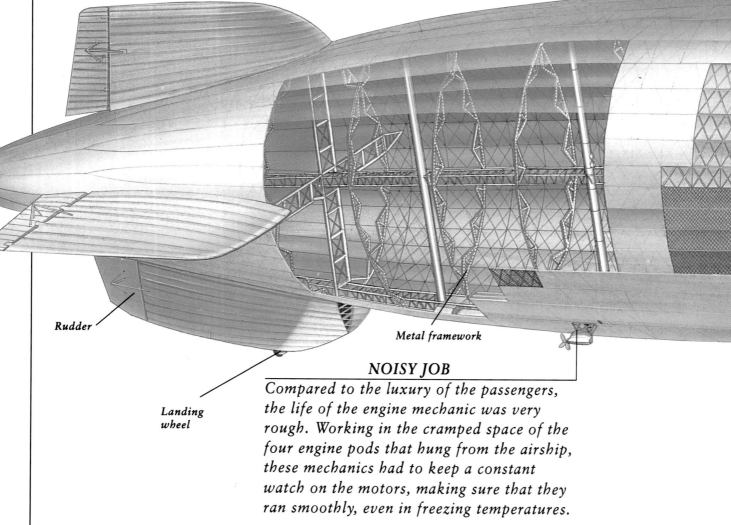

THE PROMENADE DECK

THE LAP OF LUXURY

The Hindenburg could carry up to 72 passengers in the height of luxury. The two sides of the passengers' quarters were lined with two promenade decks (left) that offered passengers views of the ground or ocean below. Next to the cabins there was a cocktail bar and even a smoking room (right).

Smoking room

Cocktail bar

Rudder

Metal framework

Landing wheel

NOISY JOB

Compared to the luxury of the passengers, the life of the engine mechanic was very rough. Working in the cramped space of the four engine pods that hung from the airship, these mechanics had to keep a constant watch on the motors, making sure that they ran smoothly, even in freezing temperatures.

DURING WORLD WAR I, airships were used for long-distance bombing raids. Once the war ended, their ability to fly huge distances made them ideal for carrying passengers quickly. They could cross the Atlantic Ocean in just over two days – faster than any ocean-going sea liner.

The largest, and one of the last to be built, was the German airship Hindenburg. It offered such a high standard of comfort that one passenger described flying in the airship as being "carried in the arms of angels."

FACTS AND FIGURES

At 804 ft (243 m) long, the Hindenburg *would dwarf a modern Boeing 747 (see page 27). In fact, the giant airship was only 78 ft (24 m) shorter than the ocean liner, Titanic. The gas cells inside the airship held an enormous 7,062,100 cubic feet (199,980 cubic meters) of hydrogen gas.*

THE HINDENBURG

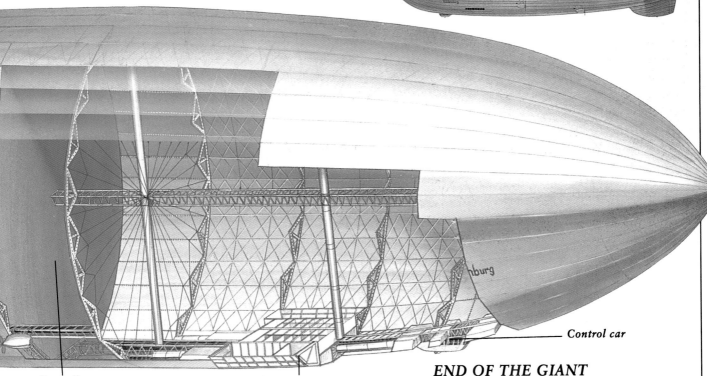

Control car

Gas cell   Passengers' quarters

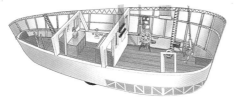

CONTROL CAR

END OF THE GIANT

On the evening of May 6, 1937 the Hindenburg *was approaching the mooring mast at Lakehurst, N.J. However, just 700 ft (200 m) short of the mooring mast, flames erupted from the airship and it fell out of the air (below). Of the 97 passengers and crew on board, 36 people died.*

The *Hindenburg* made several flights from Europe to North and South America during the 1930s. But disaster struck after one trip across the Atlantic Ocean when the hydrogen gas that kept the airship aloft exploded and sent the *Hindenburg* crashing to the ground.

THE *HINDENBURG* BURSTS INTO FLAMES

BALLOONS AND AIRSHIPS

The first free flight in an artificial device occurred in 1783. Two brothers, Jacques and Joseph Montgolfier, constructed a balloon made from linen and paper (below). A fire was built under the balloon and hot air from the fire caused the balloon to rise. The first pilots in this balloon were the Marquis d'Arlandes, a nobleman, and Jean Pilâtre, a doctor. They flew for 5 miles (8 km) over Paris. Since then, balloons and airships have been used in a great many roles, including warfare and carrying passengers. Even with today's advanced planes, there are still many jobs for these lighter-than-air machines.

MONTGOLFIERS' BALLOON

EARLY AIRSHIP DISASTERS

Aside from the Hindenburg, (see *pages 8-9*), several other airships were destroyed in accidents. One of these, the U.S. navy's airship Macon (below) crashed into the Pacific Ocean in February 1935. These accidents turned public opinion against airships. Their numbers dwindled and, by the start of World War II, they had all but disappeared.

U.S. AIRSHIP MACON

AIRSHIPS

Unlike balloons, airships can be steered and are powered by engines. Balloons have no engines and need the wind to guide them. An airship is kept aloft by special gases that are lighter than air. At first, hydrogen was used. But this gas can burst into flames and caused a number of accidents (see above).

Another gas, helium, is also lighter than air, but is safe to use as it does not burn. However, it was hard to produce and was rarely used. Today, helium is much easier to produce. Its easy availability has led to a reappearance of airships. They are now used to monitor traffic from the air and as floating advertisements (below).

MODERN AIRSHIP

Parachute vent

A LOAD OF HOT AIR

Balloons are basically large bags of hot air (left). Because the hot air inside is lighter than the air around it, the balloon rises. Passengers are carried in a basket under the balloon. Above this is a gas burner that can be turned on to heat the air in the balloon. This makes the balloon lighter, causing it to rise even higher. If the balloon has to descend, the pilot pulls on a cord. This opens a hole called the parachute vent in the top of the balloon. When this happens, hot air rushes out and the balloon sinks toward the ground.

Gas burner

Passenger basket

BREITLING ORBITER

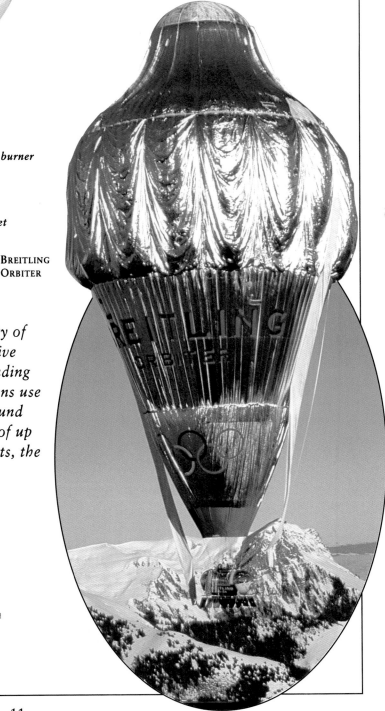

LONG-DISTANCE BALLOONING

There have been many recent tests of the ability of balloons to fly long distances. Most recently, five teams have tried to fly around the world, including Breitling Orbiter (right). To do this, the balloons use the jet streams. These are winds that blow around the world at 190 mph (300 km/h) at altitudes of up to 8.5 miles (14 km). To survive at these heights, the pilots travel inside special capsules (below).

Communications antenna

Cabin

Fuel tank

Air tank

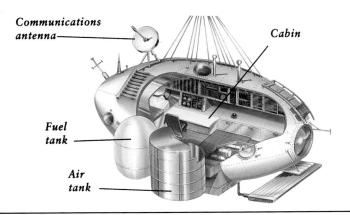

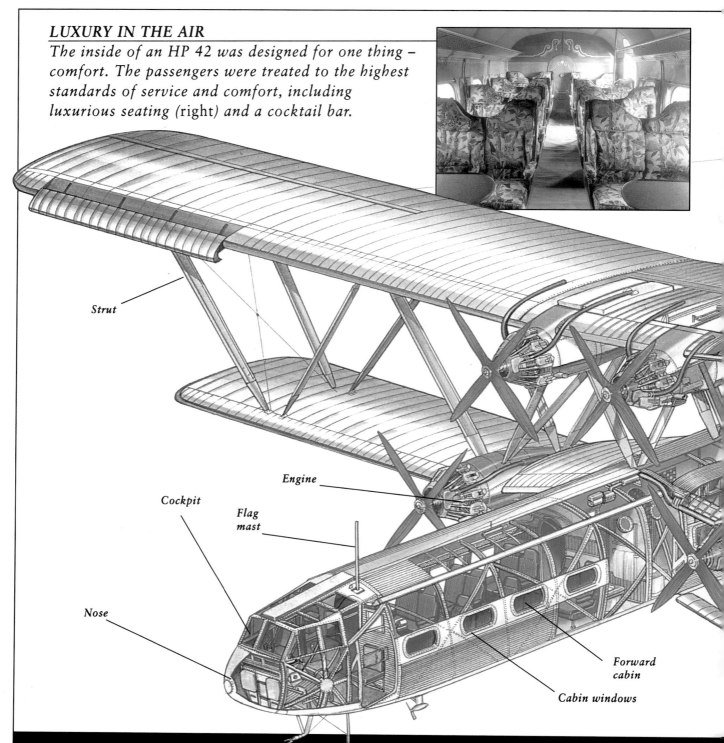

LUXURY IN THE AIR

The inside of an HP 42 was designed for one thing – comfort. The passengers were treated to the highest standards of service and comfort, including luxurious seating (right) and a cocktail bar.

Strut

Engine

Cockpit

Flag mast

Nose

Forward cabin

Cabin windows

WHEN IT WAS INTRODUCED in the early 1930s, the Handley Page HP 42 already looked out-of-date, especially when compared to other passenger aircraft of the day, such as the Ford Tri-Motor (*see* page 14) and the Lockheed Electra. However, the HP 42 had four reliable engines, sturdy construction, first-class furnishings and catering, and its interior was soundproofed effectively from the drone of its engines and the rush of passing air. Despite their slow flying speed of only 127 mph (204 km/h), the HP 42s continued flying throughout the decade, each of them flying over 12,000 hours without

THE HANDLEY PAGE HP 42

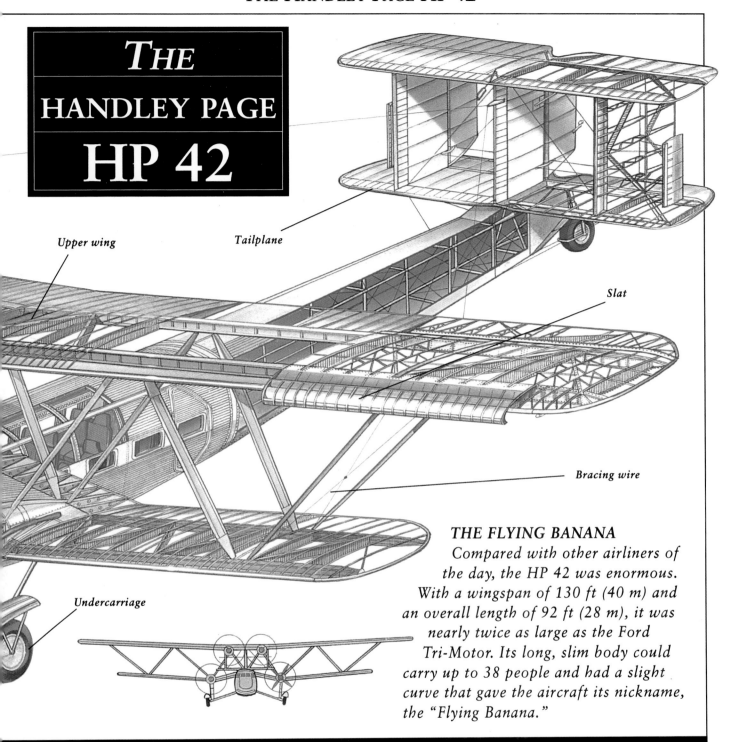

Upper wing

Tailplane

Slat

Bracing wire

Undercarriage

THE FLYING BANANA
Compared with other airliners of the day, the HP 42 was enormous. With a wingspan of 130 ft (40 m) and an overall length of 92 ft (28 m), it was nearly twice as large as the Ford Tri-Motor. Its long, slim body could carry up to 38 people and had a slight curve that gave the aircraft its nickname, the "Flying Banana."

causing a single fatality. They were even used as transport planes during World War II. Only eight of these stately aircraft were built, but they became the first commercial aircraft in the world to fly over 1 million miles (1.6 million km). The eight of them went on to fly a total of 2.3 million miles (3.7 million km)!

HANDLEY PAGE HP 42 IN FLIGHT

BETWEEN THE WARS

WINNIE MAE

FORD TRI-MOTOR

The years between the two world wars saw a massive expansion in aircraft manufacture and achievement. The first airlines appeared and began carrying cargo and passengers, first on short trips and then to the other side of the world. One of the most successful planes to appear in this period was the Ford Tri-Motor (above). The "Tin Goose," as it was nicknamed, first flew in 1926. One owner, Richard Byrd, used a Tri-Motor to fly over the South Pole, becoming the first person to fly over both poles.

FLYING AROUND THE WORLD

During this period many aviators pushed back the frontiers of flying. Between May 20–21, 1927, Charles Lindbergh (below left) became the first person to fly solo across the Atlantic Ocean in his plane, Spirit of St. Louis (bottom).

Other famous aviators of the day included Amy Johnson (right), who flew a Gypsy Moth aircraft called Jason from London to Sydney in May 1930, Amelia Earhart, who was the first woman to fly solo across the Atlantic Ocean in 1932, and Wiley Post, who was the first person to fly solo around the world in his Lockheed Vega named Winnie Mae (top). The flight took eight days, between July 15–22, 1933.

AMY JOHNSON

CHARLES LINDBERGH

Fuel tank

Engine

Cockpit

N-X-211

RYAN NVP

SPIRIT OF ST. LOUIS

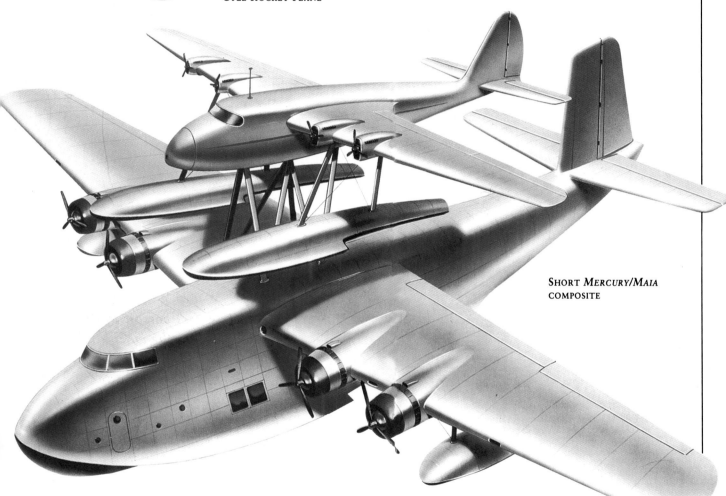

ROCKET POWER

The period between the wars saw many new and sometimes strange innovations in aircraft technology. In 1928, German designer Franz von Opel built and flew a rocket-powered plane (left). At one point it reached a speed of 100 mph (161 km/h). Opel abandoned rocket power, but rocket planes were not forgotten.

In 1967, an X-15 rocket-powered plane reached a speed of 4,534 mph (7,297 km/h).

OPEL ROCKET PLANE

SHORT *MERCURY/MAIA* COMPOSITE

SEAPLANES AND FLYING BOATS

Seaplanes and flying boats were widely used to take passengers and mail to the far-flung corners of the world during this period. The enormous Dornier Do X (right) could carry up to 170 passengers – most aircraft of the time could only carry 20 people.

An experimental attempt at increasing the range of seaplanes was the Short *Mercury/Maia* composite (above). Mercury, the smaller aircraft, was carried into the air on the back of the larger Maia plane. After takeoff, the Mercury plane broke away and continued the journey. In October 1938, the Mercury set a distance record by flying 5,998 miles (9,579 km).

DORNIER DO X

AIRCRAFT OF WORLD WAR II

Wartime is often a time of rapid technological change. During World War II, the shape of aircraft altered greatly as improved technology allowed planes to fly faster, higher, and with greater agility than ever before. However, many aircraft were still being used that were reminiscent of World War I.

FAIRY SWORDFISH

One of these was the Fairy Swordfish (above), affectionately called the "Stringbag." Despite being out-of-date before the war began and outclassed by almost every other aircraft, it was used as a torpedo bomber in many conflicts. These included the daring raid on the Italian naval base at Taranto and the hunting and sinking of the German battleship, the Bismarck.

FLIGHT OF THE CONDOR

The Focke Wolf 200C Condor (above) was described by Winston Churchill as "The scourge of the Atlantic." Originally built as a passenger aircraft, it was used as a convoy raider, and sank and crippled many Allied ships carrying troops and supplies across the Atlantic Ocean – one squadron alone sank 368,800 tons of shipping.

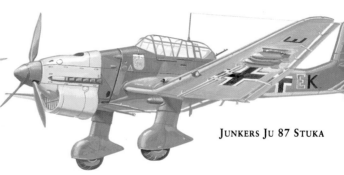

JUNKERS JU 87 STUKA

SCREAMING DIVE-BOMBER

No other aircraft has ever awakened more fear in the hearts of an enemy force than the Junkers Ju 87. Called the "Stuka," German for dive-bomber, the aircraft had sirens fitted to its undercarriage. When the plane began its steep dive to bomb a target, these sirens would create a terrifying wailing sound.

LOCKHEED P-38 LIGHTNING

FORK-TAILED DEVIL

The Lockheed P-38 Lightning (left) was designed as a bomber escort and fighter. Its chief asset was its speed – one flew across the United States in just seven hours! The Lightning proved so successful in Europe and the Pacific that enemy troops called it the "fork-tailed devil."

AIRCRAFT CARRIERS

Although they had been used in World War I, aircraft carriers came to the fore in World War II. These huge floating runways (right) were used in many important battles, including the sinking of the Bismarck (see left) and the Battles of Midway and the Coral Sea.

PLANES ON A CARRIER

DOUGLAS DC-3

The Douglas DC-3 (also known as the Dakota or the C-47 Skytrain, above) was produced in greater numbers than any other transport aircraft in history. Built for American Airlines as a passenger aircraft, it was later used as a military transport plane and to tow gliders. After the war, the aircraft continued to be used throughout the world, and some airforces and airlines still use it today.

BOEING B-29 SUPERFORTRESS

HEAVY BOMBERS

World War II saw the appearance of fleets of heavy bombers attacking enemy targets. These aircraft had to be large enough to carry huge bomb loads over vast distances. Famous bombers of the conflict included the Avro Lancaster (below) and the Boeing B-29 Superfortress (above). One Superfortress took part in possibly the most famous air raid of the war: on August 6, 1945, it dropped an atomic bomb on the Japanese city of Hiroshima.

AVRO LANCASTER

THE NORTH AMERICAN P-51 Mustang was originally moderately used as a low-level reconnaissance or ground-attack aircraft. However, by the end of the conflict it had become one of the most important weapons of World War II, escorting fleets of bombers on missions deep into the heart of enemy territory. This radical switch in roles occurred because a replacement of the engine allowed the aircraft to fly higher and faster. It could now protect bombers all the way to their targets, and the dwindling resources of the German airforce proved no match for this agile fighter.

NORTH AMERICAN P-51 MUSTANG

ENGINE POWER
The engine that revolutionized the Mustang's role was the Rolls Royce Merlin (built by license in the United States by Packard). The engine provided Mustangs with enough power to fly at 440 mph (708 km/h) and at altitudes of 42,000 ft (12,600 m).

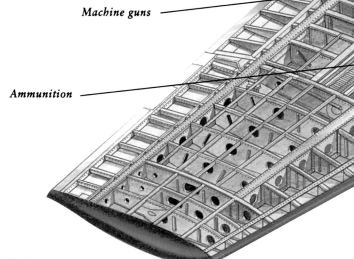

Tailplane

Tail wheel

CANOPY
Early Mustangs were fitted with a heavily framed glass roof, or canopy. Later models had large, clear, teardrop canopies that gave the pilots a much clearer view of the sky around them.

Machine guns

Ammunition

DROP TANKS
To keep up with the bomber fleets, the Mustang carried extra fuel in special drop tanks under each wing. When this extra fuel was used up, the tanks were released.

18

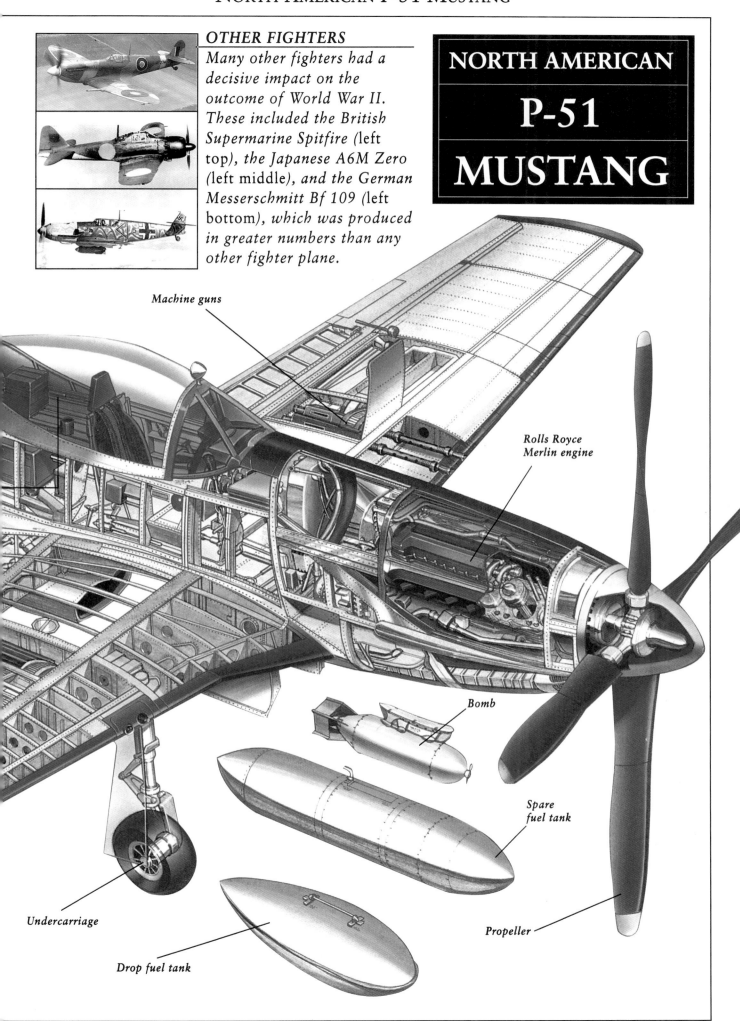

OTHER FIGHTERS

Many other fighters had a decisive impact on the outcome of World War II. These included the British Supermarine Spitfire (left top), the Japanese A6M Zero *(left middle), and the German Messerschmitt Bf 109 (left bottom),* which was produced in greater numbers than any other fighter plane.

NORTH AMERICAN
P-51
MUSTANG

Machine guns

Rolls Royce Merlin engine

Bomb

Spare fuel tank

Undercarriage

Propeller

Drop fuel tank

ROTARY-WINGED AIRCRAFT

Not all aircraft have fixed wings – that is, wings that do not move – in order to give them the lift they need to get off the ground. Others, such as helicopters and autogyros, use rotary wings, and today they are used in a wide range of roles, both military and civilian. The earliest appearance of a helicopter is in a Chinese text dating from A.D. 320. It describes a model based on a child's flying top toy. However, the first helicopter flight did not occur until 1907, when a tandem helicopter (right) built by the French inventor Paul Cornu hovered for 20 seconds at a height of 7 ft (2 m).

CORNU'S HELICOPTER

CIVIL HELICOPTERS

Helicopters are used to carry passengers on short trips. They are especially useful for landing and taking off from helicopter pads in city centers. Some, such as air ambulances, can even land in city parks or at street intersections. They can get to accidents and carry a patient to hospital more quickly than a road ambulance. Other helicopters, such as the Bell 222 (above), can carry business people to meetings without passing through congested city streets.

IGOR SIKORSKY

One of the greatest names in helicopter development was that of Igor Sikorsky. In 1940, he successfully flew a single-rotor helicopter called the VS-300 (below). This had a main rotor to provide lift and a smaller one at the rear to stop the helicopter from spinning out of control. One of his later machines, the S-64 Skycrane (right), could lift up to 18 tons of cargo, including a special pod that could carry 87 fully equipped troops, a command center, or a surgical facility.

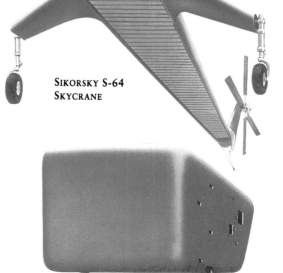

SIKORSKY S-64 SKYCRANE

SIKORSKY VS-300

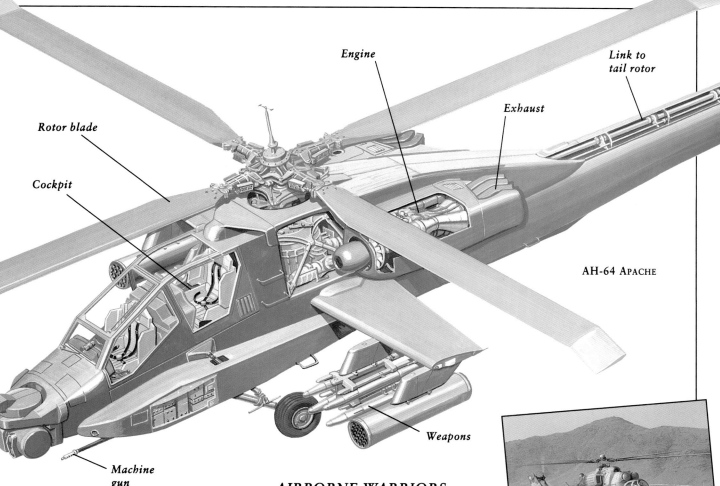

Engine

Link to
tail rotor

Exhaust

Rotor blade

Cockpit

AH-64 APACHE

Weapons

Machine
gun

AUTOGYROS

Autogyros (below right) have rotary wings just like helicopters. However, their rotors are not powered by an engine, but are sent spinning as the autogyro moves forward. (It is pushed along by a propeller behind the pilot.)
They are cheaper and easier to run than helicopters, making them very popular as fun aircraft.

AIRBORNE WARRIORS

The agility of helicopters makes them ideally suited to attack ground forces. Using natural cover they can approach a target unseen, fire at it, and then disappear quickly. Today, helicopters such as the AH-64 Apache (above) and the Mil Mi-24 Hind (above right) are fitted with very sophisticated gadgets. Pilots can use thermal-imaging devices and night sights to spot targets from a great distance in the dark.

AUTOGYRO

X-WING PLANE

Normal helicopters fly at limited speeds because vibrations created when flying quickly can damage the rotor blades. The X-wing plane (right) overcomes this because its blades stop spinning when it is airborne. To move it forward, the X-wing plane uses two powerful jet engines.

MIL MI-24 HIND

X-WING PLANE

THIS POWERFUL twin-rotor helicopter has been used for a variety of functions since it was introduced in 1961. It was first designed for the military, who used it to airlift troops and equipment to and from the battlefield and even rescue civilians – a single Chinook was able to carry 147 refugees as well as their belongings! During the Vietnam conflict, Chinooks were also used to recover some 11,500 disabled aircraft for repair or salvage.

The Chinook has also been used as a civilian passenger helicopter. It can carry up to 44 people from place to place over land or sea.

BOEING VERTOL CHINOOK

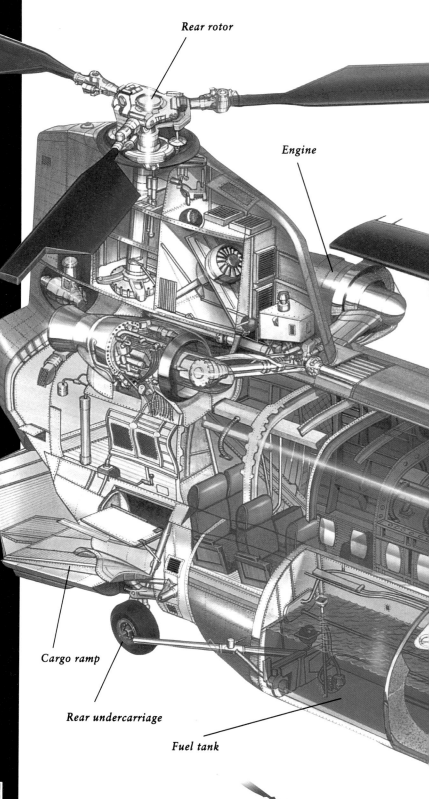

Rear rotor

Engine

Cargo ramp

Rear undercarriage

Fuel tank

POWER LIFTING
The Chinook's strength is demonstrated by its ability to lift heavy loads with its exterior hook. The powerful engines of the Chinook can lift a staggering 11.5 tons, or the weight of a heavy bulldozer!

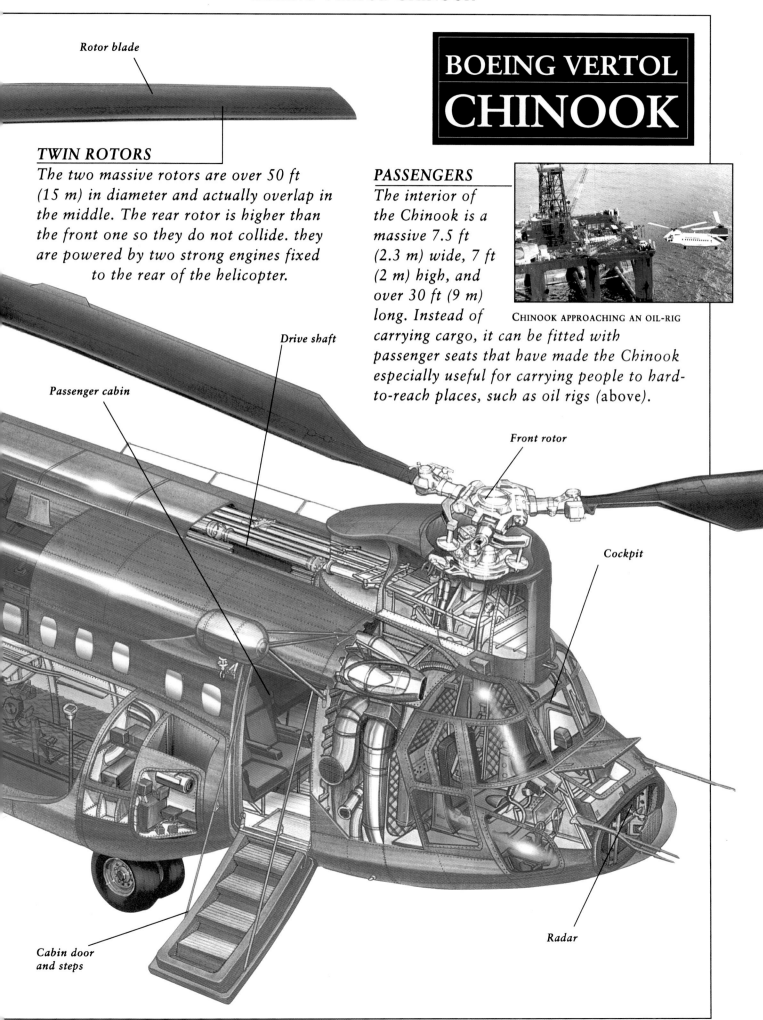

Rotor blade

BOEING VERTOL CHINOOK

TWIN ROTORS
The two massive rotors are over 50 ft (15 m) in diameter and actually overlap in the middle. The rear rotor is higher than the front one so they do not collide. they are powered by two strong engines fixed to the rear of the helicopter.

PASSENGERS
The interior of the Chinook is a massive 7.5 ft (2.3 m) wide, 7 ft (2 m) high, and over 30 ft (9 m) long. Instead of carrying cargo, it can be fitted with passenger seats that have made the Chinook especially useful for carrying people to hard-to-reach places, such as oil rigs (above).

CHINOOK APPROACHING AN OIL-RIG

Drive shaft

Passenger cabin

Front rotor

Cockpit

Cabin door and steps

Radar

THE BIRTH OF THE JET AGE

WHITTLE'S JET

The British pilot Frank Whittle (below left) was only 23 years old when he patented the turbo-jet engine in 1930. It took another 11 years to build one of his jet engines (below) and then fit it into an aircraft. In May 1941, a Gloster E.28/39 (above), an experimental jet fighter, made its first flight over the skies of Britain.

GLOSTER E.28/39

HEINKEL 178

J et propulsion involves an object being pushed forward by expanding gas. Air enters the front of a jet engine. Fans compress the air and speed up its flow before fuel is injected and ignited. This ignition causes the air to expand, forcing itself out of the back of the engine and pushing the jet forward. Jets were attractive as engines because they caused less vibration than propeller engines and created the potential to fly aircraft faster. The first jet aircraft, the Heinkel 178 (above), was built by the German physicist Hans von Ohain in August 1939.

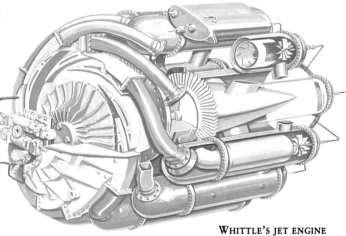

WHITTLE'S JET ENGINE

JETS OF WORLD WAR II

By the close of World War II, many of the countries fighting in the conflict had built and flown their own jet aircraft. These included the Italian Caproni-Campini CC2, the British Gloster Meteor (below), and the American Bell P-59 Airacomet. However, the world leaders in jet design were the Germans. By 1945, they had built a very successful fighter, the Messerschmitt Me262, which saw service in the last year of the war.

FRANK WHITTLE

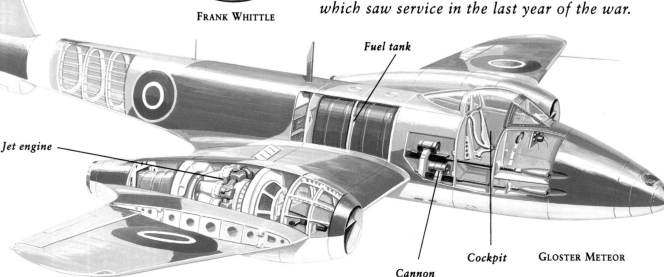

Fuel tank

Jet engine

Cockpit

GLOSTER METEOR

Cannon

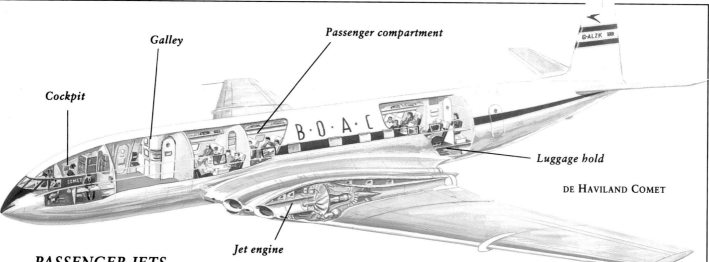

Cockpit

Galley

Passenger compartment

B.O.A.C

G-ALZK

Luggage hold

de HAVILAND COMET

Jet engine

PASSENGER JETS

The first jet airliner was the de Haviland Comet (above). It entered service in 1952 when a Comet carrying 36 passengers took off for Rome. However, early problems led to a pause in the plane's production, during which time other companies had developed their own jet airliners, for example the Boeing 707.

BOMBERS

Still in use today, the Boeing B-52 Stratofortress (below) followed on from where aircraft such as the B-29 Superfortress (see page 17) left off. More powerful engines meant bombers could fly farther and carry a greater bomb load. The Stratofortress was the culmination of this – its wingspan is longer than the Wright Brothers' first flight (see page 5).

F-86 SABRE

JET VERSUS JET

The first air-to-air combat between jet fighters occurred during the Korean War (1950-1953). On November 8, 1950, North Korean MiG-15 fighters attacked a group of American bombers that were escorted by Lockheed F-80 Shooting Stars. However, air combat during the Korean War was dominated by the clash between the MiG-15 and another jet, the North American F-86 Sabre (left). These planes first met in combat on December 17, 1950. At the end of the war, Sabres had shot down 757 MiGs with the loss of only 103 Sabres.

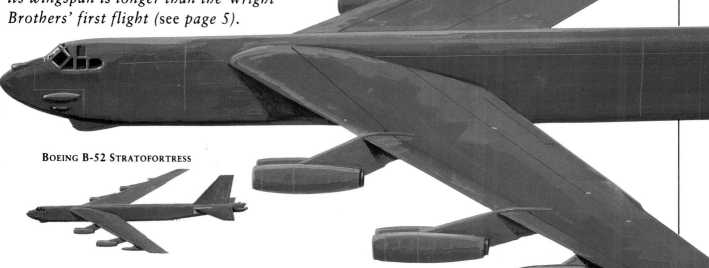

BOEING B-52 STRATOFORTRESS

CIVIL AVIATION

BOEING 307 STRATOLINER

The increase in civilian air travel after World War II, along with the development of jet engines and more comfortable aircraft, has opened up the skies. Today, the busiest airports handle over 60 million people each year. They have runways that can be nearly 3 miles (5 km) long to handle passenger aircraft that can carry over 600 people. All of these flights are controlled from flight centers that are packed with the latest technology (right). Much has changed since the days of the 1940s and 1950s, when airports were tiny compared with today's giants.

TRAVELING IN COMFORT

By flying at high altitudes, aircraft can travel above bad weather, making the flight less bumpy for passengers. However, the air is thin and very cold at these heights. Cabin pressurization and heating made flying at these heights more comfortable. The first airliner to use these was the Boeing 307 Stratoliner (above). This could carry up to 33 passengers in comfort – some even had beds for passengers to sleep in!

PROPELLERS

Propellers are still used on many passenger aircraft around the world. They are especially useful at inner-city airports where it is important to use quiet aircraft to minimize disturbance. One aircraft that still uses propellers is the de Haviland Canada Dash-7 (below). It can carry 54 people and only needs a runway that is 2,300 ft (700 m) long to take off.

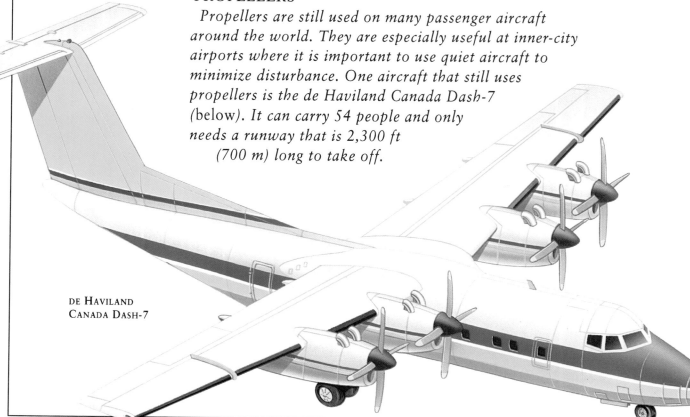

DE HAVILAND CANADA DASH-7

MODERN AIRPORTS

Today's airports need to be big to handle the huge numbers of people that use them (right). The world's busiest airport, O'Hare Airport in Chicago, handled 909,593 aircraft movements in 1996, and used by 69,153,528 passengers.

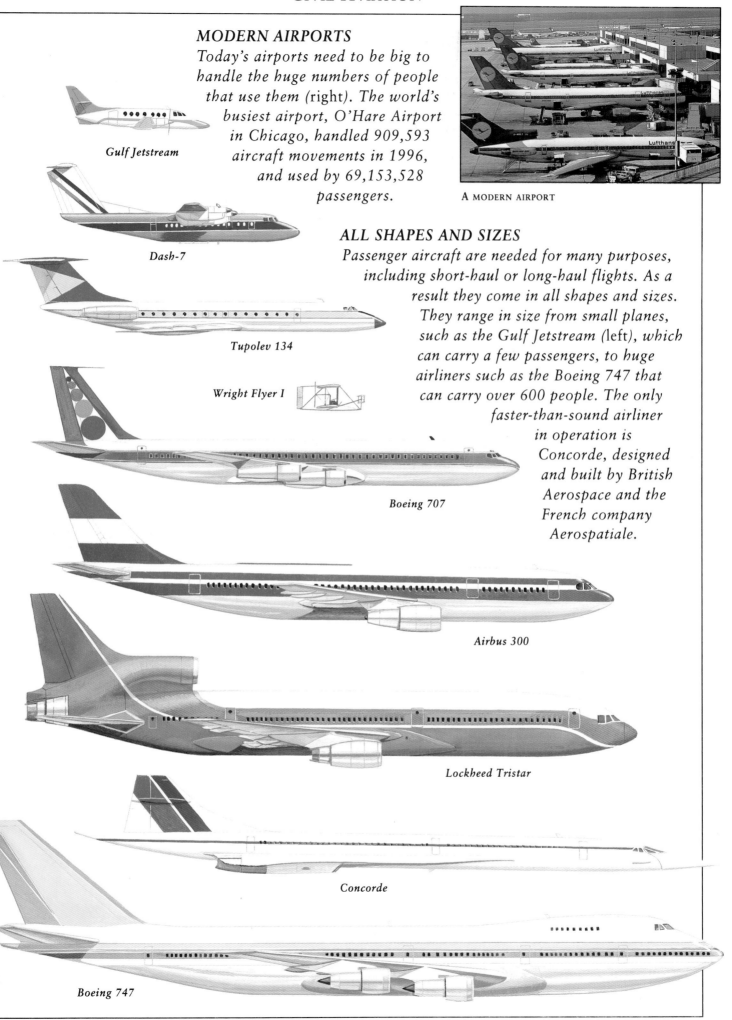

A MODERN AIRPORT

Gulf Jetstream

Dash-7

Tupolev 134

Wright Flyer I

ALL SHAPES AND SIZES

Passenger aircraft are needed for many purposes, including short-haul or long-haul flights. As a result they come in all shapes and sizes. They range in size from small planes, such as the Gulf Jetstream (left), which can carry a few passengers, to huge airliners such as the Boeing 747 that can carry over 600 people. The only faster-than-sound airliner in operation is Concorde, designed and built by British Aerospace and the French company Aerospatiale.

Boeing 707

Airbus 300

Lockheed Tristar

Concorde

Boeing 747

BOEING 777

COCKPIT OF A 777

FOLDING WINGS
Some models of the 777 are built with folding wing tips. At speeds of less than 56 mph (90 km/h), the outer 21.5 ft (6.5 m) can be folded up, allowing the plane to fit into narrower taxiways and gates.

Flap

Wing

Engine

GRAND VIEW
The 777 is fitted with three cameras, positioned on the front edges of the tailplane and under the body of the plane. Displayed in the cockpit (above) these give the crew a view of the front wheel and the underside of both wings. This is particularly helpful when taxiing to takeoff or from landing.

Cockpit

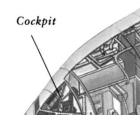

Engine

FOR OVER THIRTY YEARS, the Boeing 747 (*see* page 27) has been the mainstay of many airlines' long-haul flights, carrying up to 566 passengers on transcontinental flights. However, with many 747s reaching their retirement age, airlines have been searching for a replacement. One answer lies in the Boeing 777-300, the largest twin-engined aircraft ever built. This massive jet is set to replace the now aging fleet of humpbacked 747s. The Boeing 777-300 can be fitted to carry 550 passengers, roughly the

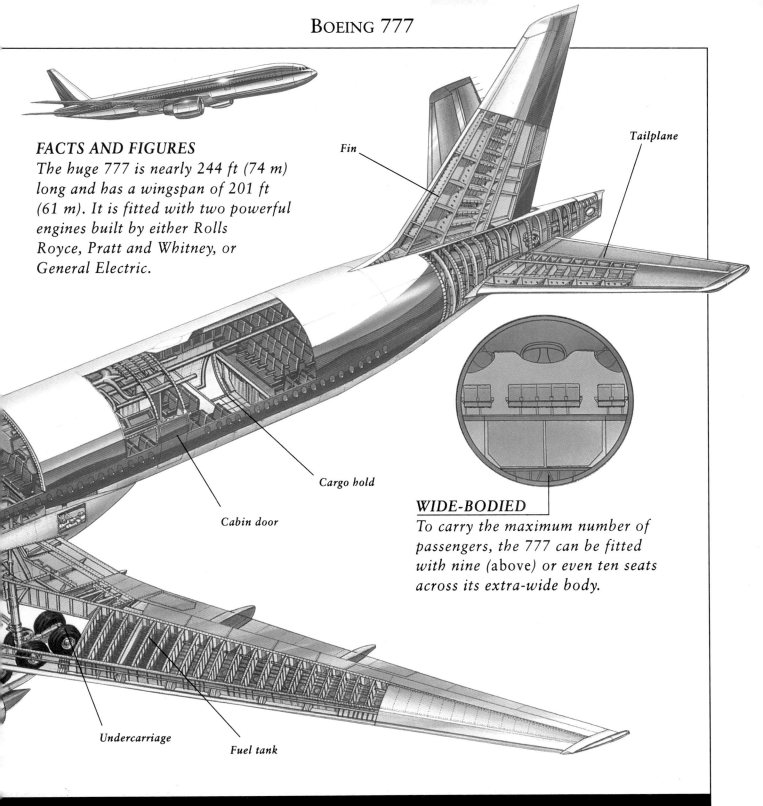

FACTS AND FIGURES

The huge 777 is nearly 244 ft (74 m) long and has a wingspan of 201 ft (61 m). It is fitted with two powerful engines built by either Rolls Royce, Pratt and Whitney, or General Electric.

Fin

Tailplane

Cargo hold

Cabin door

Undercarriage

Fuel tank

WIDE-BODIED

To carry the maximum number of passengers, the 777 can be fitted with nine (above) or even ten seats across its extra-wide body.

same as the 747. However, the real savings come in the operating costs of the newer plane. Able to fly between continents, the Boeing 777-300 uses one-third less fuel than the Boeing 747 and has maintenance costs that are 40 percent less than its predecessor.

BOEING 777

FLYING FOR FUN

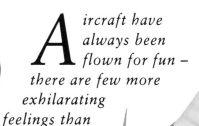

GeeBee Sportster

Aircraft have always been flown for fun – there are few more exhilarating feelings than being set free from the restrictions of living on the ground. Recreational flying can take many forms. These include racing, stunt flying, or simply flying for sheer pleasure. Air races were very popular in the 1930s. One plane that dominated air racing during this period was the GeeBee Sportster (above). It was built solely for speed, with an enormous engine bolted onto a small body. It won the much sought after Thompson Trophy in 1932 and set a new airspeed record of 296 mph (477 km/h)!

DO-IT-YOURSELF FLYING
During the 1930s, the development of the Pou-de-Ciel (below) started a craze for do-it-yourself flying. This strange-looking plane came in kit form with instructions.

The enthusiasm for kit planes has never dwindled and today there are many do-it-yourself fliers around the world.

POU-DE-CIEL

SKY-WALKING
After World War I, many pilots who had flown during the conflict took to showing their flying skills at special air shows. Here they would swoop low over gasping crowds with assistants standing on the wings of the plane. These assistants would also undertake feats of bravery that included walking the length of a wing and even jumping between planes high above the ground!

WING-WALKING

SUPERMARINE S6B

SEAPLANES

*First flown
in 1912, the
Schneider Trophy
was an annual
competition for seaplanes.
It was decided that the
nation whose seaplanes won
the race three times in a row
would win the trophy outright. The prize
was finally captured in 1931, when a
Supermarine S6B (right) won the race for
Britain. The S6B flew at 340 mph (548 km/h);
the technology from this was used to develop
one of the best fighter planes of World War II,
the Spitfire (see page 19).*

HANG GLIDER

GLIDER

GLIDING

*Gliders (left) use
currents of rising warm air
to stay aloft. They use
these currents to lift them up before
gliding away and finding another rising warm
current. To get airborne, they can use a small
motor that is turned off once in the air, a land-
based pulley, or they can be towed behind an
airplane and then released. Another form
of gliding involves a person being
suspended in a harness beneath
a wing. This is called
hang gliding (above).*

MICROLIGHTS

*One of the most popular and cheapest forms
of flying today is in a microlight (below).
The pilot sits in a small, open cockpit under
a wing. The power comes from a small
engine, and the pilot steers the aircraft by
moving the wing, just like a hang glider.*

ROCKET PACK

*Attempts are always being
tried to make flying easier for
everybody. One proposal was the
personal rocket pack (right). Fitted
to the back of a person, this would
offer the flier the means to
fly from place to place above
congested roads without the
need for airports or a runway.
However, the idea proved too
costly and the jet pack could carry
only enough fuel to last for a few seconds.*

ROCKET PACK

MICROLIGHT

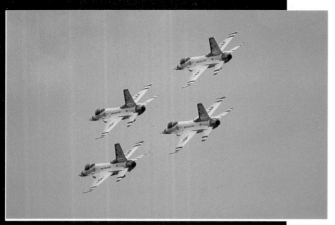

THUNDERBIRDS DISPLAY TEAM

TOO CLOSE FOR COMFORT

A show by the Thunderbirds can have 30 different maneuvers involving up to six aircraft. These maneuvers can include maximum-performance turns and precision diamond flying (left), in which four aircraft fly loops and rolls in a diamond formation with the tips of their wings as little as 1.5 ft (45 cm) apart!

ALMOST EVERY AIR FORCE has its own aerobatic display team, to show off the skills of its pilots, the technology of its aircraft, and to attract new recruits. The Thunderbird display team of the United States Air Force tours the world showing its breathtaking flying skills to thousands of people every year. Since they were formed over 40 years ago, in May 1953, the Thunderbirds have performed in more than 3,300 airshows in front of 275 million people. In that time they have flown a variety of jets, including the F-84 Thunderstreak and the F-4 Phantom, before settling on the plane they fly today, the F-16 Fighting Falcon.

SKILL IN THE AIR

Pilots for aerobatic display teams need to be extremely skillful fliers. Each flier chosen from the applicants for a position with the Thunderbirds must have at least 1,000 flying hours in high-performance aircraft!

Cockpit

Radar

FLY-BY-WIRE

The F-16 Fighting Falcon was the first production aircraft to have fly-by-wire technology, in which instructions are carried from the pilot to the aircraft's control surfaces (e.g. the rudder) by electrical wires rather than the cables and linkage controls used in earlier aircraft. As a result, the pilots need less strength to move the controls and they can fly the plane more easily. This allows the F-16 to make maneuvers that other planes cannot.

AEROBATIC TEAMS

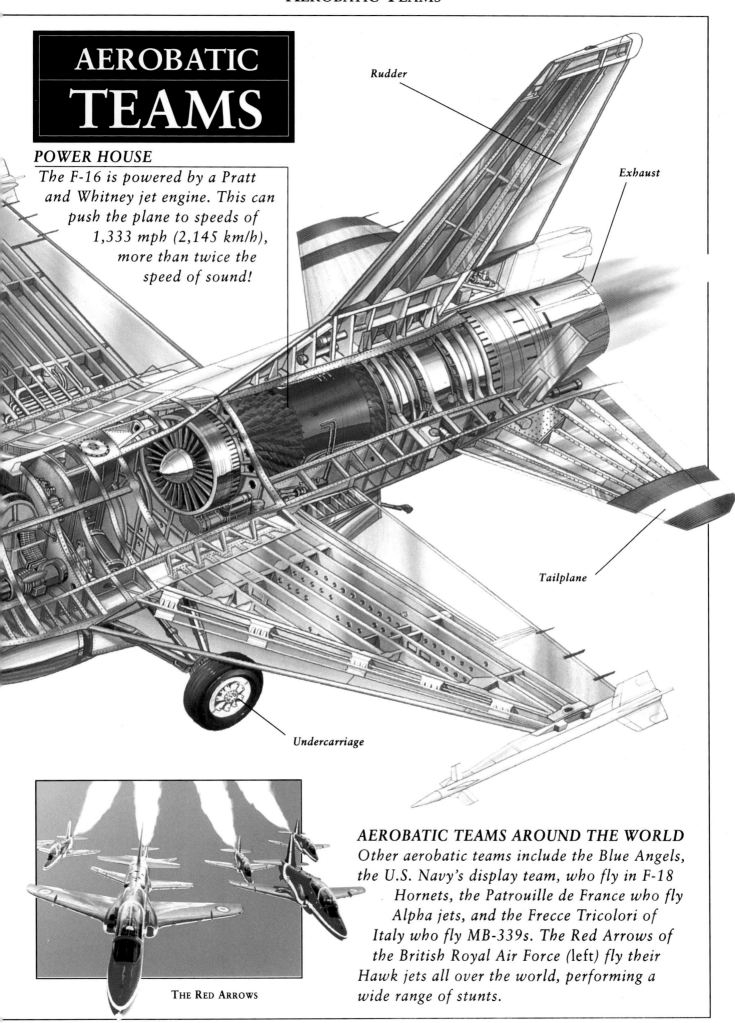

POWER HOUSE

The F-16 is powered by a Pratt and Whitney jet engine. This can push the plane to speeds of 1,333 mph (2,145 km/h), more than twice the speed of sound!

Rudder

Exhaust

Tailplane

Undercarriage

THE RED ARROWS

AEROBATIC TEAMS AROUND THE WORLD

Other aerobatic teams include the Blue Angels, the U.S. Navy's display team, who fly in F-18 Hornets, the Patrouille de France who fly Alpha jets, and the Frecce Tricolori of Italy who fly MB-339s. The Red Arrows of the British Royal Air Force (left) fly their Hawk jets all over the world, performing a wide range of stunts.

BOMB LOAD

The B-2 can carry over 18 tons of bombs. The bombs are stored on a rotating magazine (below) – when one warhead is dropped, the magazine rotates to allow the next bomb to be released.

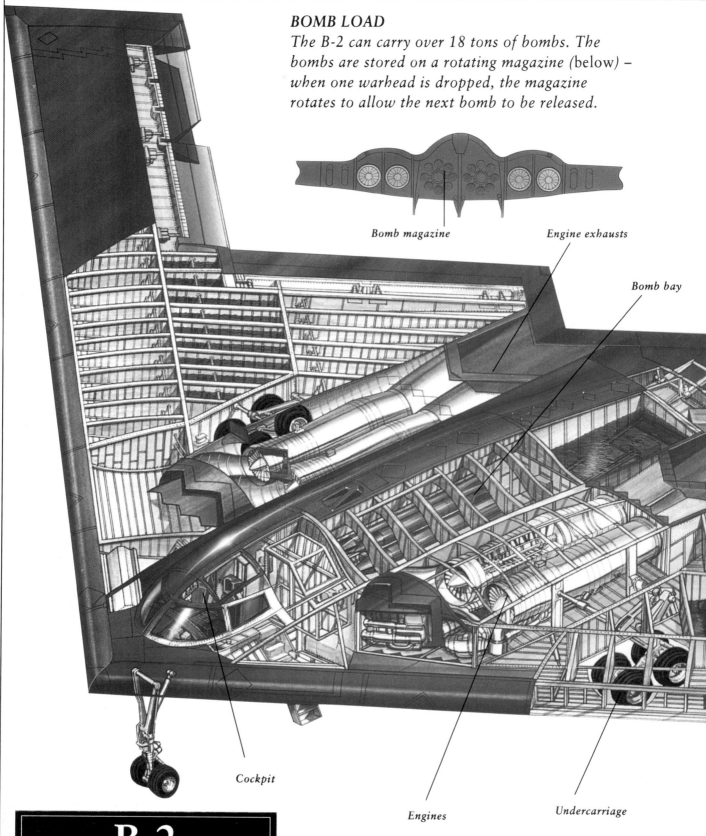

Bomb magazine

Engine exhausts

Bomb bay

Cockpit

Engines

Undercarriage

B-2 STEALTH BOMBER

CREW NUMBERS

Unlike earlier bombers, the B-2 needs only two people to fly it (however, there is space for a third). The swing-wing B-1B needs a crew of four, while the giant B-52 (see page 25) needs a total of five personnel to operate it.

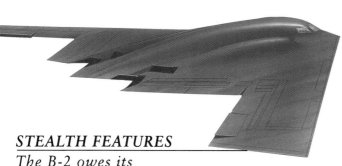

B-2 STEALTH BOMBER AT NIGHT

STEALTH FEATURES

The B-2 owes its "invisible" qualities to its unique design and paint coating. Both have been developed to scatter and absorb radar signals rather than reflect them back to a receiving antenna. The heat from the engines is also concealed by using specially designed exhausts. However, the B-2 has encountered several problems regarding its stealth capabilities – perhaps most notably when early versions became visible to radar when they got wet in the rain.

STEALTH TECHNOLOGY gives armed forces the ability to attack enemy positions without being "spotted." Stealth planes and ships use advanced technology to try and hide themselves from enemy radar, infrared (heat), and acoustic (sound) detectors. This technology can involve special body shapes and paint coverings (*see left*).

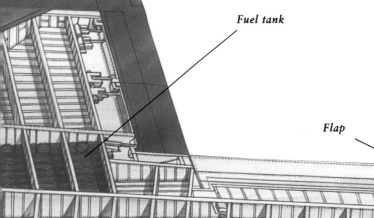

Fuel tank

Flap

FIGHTER

The Lockheed F-117 (right) is the only stealth aircraft to have been used in active service. During the Gulf War, they were used to attack targets and get away without being detected. Like the B-2, the F-117 relies on its design to disrupt radar signals and the shape of its exhausts to hide the heat from its engines.

F-117 STEALTH FIGHTER

By avoiding detection, these planes minimize the danger to the pilots flying them. The first stealth plane was the F-117 Stealth Fighter, used in the Gulf War of 1991. This was followed by the larger B-2 Stealth Bomber.

THE FUTURE

CITIES IN THE SKY

The next millennium could see the return of huge airships. However, the new generation of airships may dwarf the monsters of sixty years ago. Suggestions include a huge airship (below), 1.6 miles (2.5 km) long, 0.6 miles (1 km) wide, capable of carrying 3,500 people and 30,000 tons of cargo. It would be powered by over 160 engines. Too big to be housed in any hangar, the airship would be built in a specially roofed-off section of the Grand Canyon before taking off and staying in the air indefinitely. Passengers and cargo would be ferried up in shuttle aircraft that could land on a small runway on top of the airship!

The challenge to designers in the future is a daunting one. Increasing numbers of people are looking to fly more often, more cheaply, and farther than ever before.

One answer might be a ground-effect plane (right). Its wings would trap a layer of air on top of which the plane would ride. Other suggestions include airships that are the size of small cities, planes with no pilots, and even reusable spacecraft or space planes that leave the atmosphere altogether and orbit around the Earth.

GROUND-EFFECT PLANE

CITY-SIZED AIRSHIP

STEALTH
AIRCRAFT

INVISIBLE FLYING

Using today's new stealth
technology, the next
generation of military
aircraft will fly through
the air totally invisible to radar
(left). It may even be possible
to replace human pilots with remotely guided
systems or completely independent
computers.

ROBOT PLANES

Although they might sound
as if they are to be in the
future, robot planes are
with us already (right).
They are mainly used
by the military for
observation flights over
enemy territory, to
eliminate the need to risk
a pilot's life.

ROBOT PLANE

SPACE PLANE

SPACE PLANES

Scientists have known for a
long time that flying in space offers
many possibilities for commercial flight.
Above the atmosphere, space planes (left)
would encounter little or no friction and could fly
at speeds of Mach 26 (twenty-six times the speed
of sound – about ten times faster than a speeding
bullet!). A trip from London to New York could be
achieved in under 30 minutes!

THE NEXT SHUTTLE

With the current space shuttle
nearly 20 years old, NASA is
eager to develop a
replacement. The proposed
X-33 (right) will be a fully
reusable orbital shuttle. In
the future, it will carry spare
parts and astronauts up to the
International Space Station
that will be built over the
next ten years.

X-33 NEXT-GENERATION SHUTTLE

GLOSSARY

Aerobatics
The art of performing stunts in the air. These can be performed by a single plane or even a whole team of aircraft.

Airship
A powered flying machine that is kept in the air by using a huge bag filled with lighter-than-air gas. This gas is usually helium, although explosive hydrogen was used in the past.

Autogyro
A flying machine that, like a helicopter, is kept in the air by a rotor. However, unlike a helicopter, the rotor on an autogyro is not spun by an engine. Instead, it rotates freely as the autogyro moves through the air.

Biplane
An aircraft that has two wings, usually with one above another.

Bomber
A military plane that is specifically designed to carry bombs and drop them on an enemy target.

Canopy
The covering to a cockpit, usually made from glass.

Fighter
A military plane that is specifically designed to attack and destroy other aircraft.

Hot-air balloon
A flying machine that is kept aloft by hot air that is heated by a gas burner. Unlike airships, hot-air balloons do not have engines and propellers to move them about. Instead they use winds.

Jet engine
An engine that moves a plane by creating a jet of fast-moving gases that pushes the plane forward.

Monoplane
An aircraft with only one wing.

Propeller
A device made up from a number of specially shaped, angled blades. When these blades are sent spinning, usually by an engine, they create a force that moves an aircraft along.

Reconnaissance
Examining a region of ground, usually to detect the position or strength of an enemy.

Rotary engine
An engine where the cylinders are arranged around the propeller shaft.

Rotary-winged aircraft
An aircraft where a rotor or number of rotors, rather than a fixed wing, provide the lift to get the aircraft off the ground.

Seaplane
An aircraft that can take off and land on water. These planes are fitted with a number of floats instead of wheels.

Stealth
The ability of a body to move about without being detected. Stealth planes use special body shapes and paints to avoid being spotted by enemy radar.

Triplane
An aircraft that has three wings arranged one on top of the other.

Undercarriage
The landing gear of an aircraft. It can be made up of wheels, floats, or even skis.

Wingspan
The distance between the tips of opposite wings.

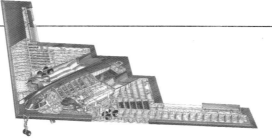

CHRONOLOGY

1783 Two French brothers, Jacques and Joseph Montgolfier build the first hot-air balloon. It was flown for 5 miles (8 km) over the city of Paris.

1874 French inventor, Felix du Temple, succeeds in making a short flying hop from a metal ramp in his steam-powered plane.

1903 The Wright brothers make the first controlled powered flight in their plane, the Wright Flyer I. Their first flight lasts only 12 seconds.

1904 English inventor Horatio Phillips claims to make a powered flight of 500 ft (150 m). This was never confirmed.

1907 Paul Cornu, a French inventor, makes the first flight in a helicopter. His tandem helicopter hovers at a height of 7 ft (2 m) for 20 seconds.

1909 Louis Blériot, a French aviator, makes the first plane crossing of the English Channel in his Blériot XI monoplane.

1913 Igor Sikorsky builds the first passenger plane, the enormous Sikorsky "Le Grand."

1918 Baron Manfred von Richthofen, also known as the Red Baron, is shot down and killed.

1919 Two British pilots, Captain John Alcock and Arthur Brown, become the first people to make a non-stop flight across the Atlantic Ocean.

1927 U.S. pilot, Charles Lindbergh, becomes the first person to fly solo across the Atlantic Ocean. He makes the journey in his plane, *Spirit of St. Louis*.

1928 German designer, Franz von Opel, builds and flies a rocket-powered plane to a speed of 100 mph (161 km/h).

1928 Richard Byrd becomes the first person to fly over both poles, when his Ford Tri-Motor takes him over Antarctica.

1930 Amy Johnson flies her Tiger Moth airplane, called *Jason*, from London, England, to Sydney, Australia.

1931 A British seaplane, the Supermarine S6B, wins the Schneider Trophy outright for Britain.

1932 Amelia Earhart becomes the first woman to fly solo across the Atlantic Ocean.

1933 Wiley Post becomes the first person to fly solo around the world in his plane, a Lockheed Vega called *Winnie Mae*.

1935 The U.S. Navy airship, *Macon*, crashes into the Pacific Ocean.

1937 The *Hindenburg* bursts into flames and crashes just short of its mooring mast at Lakehurst, N.J.

1939 German scientist Hans von Ohain builds and flies the world's first jet plane, a Heinkel 178.

1940 Igor Sikorsky builds and flies his first helicopter, the VS-300.

1945 A Boeing B-29 Superfortress drops an atomic bomb on Hiroshima.

1947 American pilot, Chuck Yeager, becomes the first person to fly faster than the speed of sound. This is achieved in a specially built rocket plane, the Bell X-1.

1950 MiG-15s and Lockheed F-80 Shooting Stars meet in the first combat between jet fighters.

1952 The world's first jet airliner, the de Haviland Comet, enters service.

1969 Concorde, the world's first supersonic jet airliner, makes its maiden flight. It remains the only passenger plane to fly faster than the speed of sound.

1991 During the Gulf War, the Lockheed F-117 Stealth Fighter becomes the first stealth aircraft to see combat.

1997-1998 Several teams of balloonists try to become the first people to fly around the world in a hot-air balloon.

INDEX

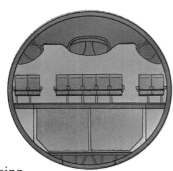
Photographic credits:

Abbreviations: t-top, m-middle, b-bottom, r-right, l-left

All the pictures in this book are supplied by Phillip Jarret
    except the following pages:
    Pages 8, 9 & 13 – Solution Pictures. 10b, 11, 21 both,
    28, 29, 31 both, & 37 both – Frank Spooner Pictures.
    14tr & 33 – Castrol Oil. 20 – Spectrum Color Library.
    22 & Back cover – Paul Nightingale. 26b – The Civil
Aviation Authority. 27 – Lufthansa. 32 – Aviation Picture
Library. 36 – Prof. C.L. Owen, Illinois Institute of Technology.